BRITISH COLUMBIA calling

British Columbia is partly real,
partly myth. It is the Province some
say has never joined the rest of
Canada and it generates intense
loyalty from its citizens.

It is also a land of incredible
contrasts — rain forest to high
desert, silent snow to pounding surf,
trees centuries old rising from mossy
forest floors to performers in a
sophisticated night club, a fiery lead
furnace to a grizzled rancher.

The words always seem
inadequate to portray the fabulous
country, but the pictures can sometimes unfold its splendour, as they do
in the following pages.

This book can be used in many
ways — by the British Columbian
who wants to savour the beauties of
his own special place, to entice Aunt
Nellie from overseas, to tempt the
tourists or even to make other
Canadians jealous. Whichever the
reader chooses, the call of British
Columbia is irresistible.

In its journey across Canada, the
sun finally sets in the deep waters
of the Pacific; the cry of the
lonely seagull and the splash of
the tide echo the sounds of
the passing day.

Like her seagulls, British Columbia,
in her solitary grandeur, soars high
above the other provinces, separated
by the snowy spines of the Rockies
in the hush of her eternal forest.

The seagull in its undulating flight
portrays the free spirit of her people.
The evergreen splendour haunts, lures,
moulds the character of her citizens
who live in this vast land.

Ted Czolowski

BRITISH COLUMBIA
calling

Photography / Ted Czolowski
Text / Mary Moon

Foam and surf, by G.W. Bates.

Evergreen Splendour

Geologists today tell us that British Columbia came into being more than 600 million years ago, before the Cambrian period. At one pre-historic time, gigantic reptiles crashed through B.C. forests of huge ferns and splashed through tropical swamps full of insect life.

Long before the first human being appeared in what is now Canada's third-largest province, red hot lava spewed out of fissures in the ground, changing the terrain once more, trapping the ancient forests inside the cooling rocks for present-day people to marvel at. Lava flows of long ago can be seen in many places in the south and interior of this Province.

Until roughly 25 million years ago, there was a huge land mass west of the present coastline of British Columbia. Its name was Cascadia and, like the legendary continent of Atlantis, one day it sank beneath the waves leaving nothing behind but tantalizing stories. Of Cascadia there remain the mountain tops we now call the offshore islands, the largest of which are Vancouver Island and the Queen Charlottes.

Windstorms, freezing and thawing action on the high ground as B.C.'s climate gradually cooled around ten million years ago, helped to carve magnificent chains of stony peaks running from north to south, making this Province an almost endless Switzerland. The grandeur of the skyline is due to the fact that the geological tantrums causing it are comparatively "recent," as geologists reckon time. This mostly-mountainous territory rises from sea level to 15,300 feet at the top of Mount Fairweather, part of the St. Elias range on the B.C.-Alaska border.

It has been said: "The mountains are here today, they were not here yesterday, they will not be here tomorrow." This is true of B.C.'s mountains largely because of the heavy precipitation and mighty rivers which carry away this Province, fragment by fragment, to the Pacific and Arctic oceans. There are three main river systems — the Fraser-Thompson-Nechako, which drains almost the whole central part, the Peace-Parsnip-Finlay in the north, and the Columbia-Kootenay-Okanagan, which reaches into the southeast corner and a portion of the south central region.

Half the population of B.C. lives on the Fraser River delta, which in prehistoric times lay under nearly six hundred feet of sea water and later was depressed one thousand feet by the weight of the ice age blanket. Today it boasts some of the richest farmland on earth and the city of Greater Vancouver, home of one million people.

British Columbia possesses almost 7,000 square miles of fresh water — more than any other Canadian province. Chief of the many natural finger lakes filling beds carved long and narrow by the glaciers of the ice age is Atlin Lake, with 217 square miles in B.C. and 28 in the Yukon. Other giants are Teslin, Babine, Kootenay, Okanagan, Stuart, Shuswap, Quesnel, Takla and Francois. The very largest body of water is man-made Lake Williston behind W.A.C. Bennett Dam — it covers 680 square miles.

Glaciers escaping westward at the end of the ice age gouged out deep coastal valleys into which the ocean rushed as the ice melted away, creating the "drowned fiord system" which can be seen between the Portland Canal in the far north to Howe Sound in the far south. One fiord, consisting of Otter Passage and Gardner Canal on the northern coast, measures 120 miles.

In startling contrast to the mild wetness of the coastal rain forests and the eternal snows on certain B.C. summits are the desert conditions found in the south-central parts of the Province. This area offers two thousand hours of sunshine every year. A narrow strip of land thirty miles long, on either side of of the Okanagan River between Penticton and the U.S. border, and the Similkameen Valley south of Keremeos, have hot dry summers and less than eight inches of rain a year.

Antelope bush, sagebrush, tumbleweed, strongly-spiked prickly pear cactus, whitetail jackrabbits, turtles and rattle-snakes can be found there. There are even rippling desert sand dunes beside Osoyoos Lake. Sagebrush, cactus, smoke trees and tumbleweed can be seen throughout the Okanagan Valley too and even along the historic Cariboo Highway which led to the famed gold fields.

British Columbia is a land of infinite variety and distinctive areas. Differing completely from the Okanagan are the Kootenays and the Cariboo with their special blend of beauty and interest. Besides its many "little Switzerlands" the former has Nelson, "Queen City" of the Kootenays; the tourist centre of Cranbrook and restored Fort Steele; the smelter city of Trail; Kimberley, of Sullivan Mine renown; and Fernie, coming into its own again as "King of Coal." The Cariboo and Chilcotin have their particular allure of rolling grasslands and big skies, and the myth that they are only "a state of mind." And the northeast has its bustling communities of Dawson Creek, Chetwynd and Fort St. John.

But it is for her 138,400,000 acres of forest — nearly sixty per cent of the terrain — that British Columbia is famous. This is the magic land of the woodsmen, nature lovers, conser-vationists and refugees from the rat race. The forest primeval. The evergreen splendour.

(Right) Spring comes to Beacon Hill Park in Victoria, capital of British Columbia.

6   *(Overleaf) Coastal scene near Ucluelet on the west coast of Vancouver Island.*

Sea anemones in a typical ebbtide pool in Pacific Rim National Park.

11

Pacific Rim Park

One of the newest national parks in Western Canada is Pacific Rim National Park, almost half-way up Vancouver Island's west coast. As money and lands become available, the park will be developed in three stages, starting with the Long Beach area between Ucluelet and Tofino. The second phase is a group of islands at the entrance to Barkley Sound. The third stage covers the area between Bamfield and Port Renfrew, including a famous life-saving trail. In strategic places, there will be exhibits to help visitors understand the natural state of the tidal waters, rocks and islets, beach and rain forest. Commercial enterprises and permanent living quarters are forbidden in this Eden.

(Upper Left) Long Beach, on Vancouver Island's western shores.
(Lower Left) Drifting sand dunes of Long Beach.
(Right) Rock plants, sea lions and sea anemones in Pacific Rim National Park.

13

Barkley Sound

The first white woman to see Pacific North West America and set foot in British Columbia was the seventeen-year-old bride of British fur-trader Captain Charles William Barkley, in 1787. In the sound on Vancouver Island's southwest coast which he named after himself are channels called Loudoun and Imperial Eagle — the two names of his ship — and Trevor, Mrs. Barkley's maiden name. The former Frances Hornby Trevor wrote that they traded with Indians in Friendly Cove *(see p. 40)*, went exploring southwards, naming Wickaninnish Bay for the local Indian chief, Frances Island and Hornby Peak. They discovered a channel which they concluded must be the lost Strait of Juan de Fuca, and that is what Captain Barkley called it.

Barkley Sound is a graveyard for ships (Above).
Racing water between the rocks (Right) drives
many a vessel to its destruction.

14

Okanagan Valley

David Stuart, fur-trader, discovered the Okanagan Valley and
its 80-mile-long lake in 1811, when
he led the first known party of
white people into the area. The
name of *Kelowna*, the valley's
largest community, means "grizzly
bear" in the Indian language. City
population jumped overnight
in 1973, from 20,000 to 40,000,
when outlying areas were included.
Penticton's Indian name,
"Pentk-tn," means "always place"
or permanent camp. The population numbers almost 20,000.
Vernon is named for the Vernon
brothers, Forbes George and
Charles, pioneer ranchers. The
Indians knew it as "Nintle-moos-
chin" or "jumping-over place."
More than 13,000 people live there.

Dry in places as a desert (Left)
the Valley is a mass of bloom in spring.
(Above) Spring sunflowers.
(Right) Cherry, pear and apple blossoms.
(Overleaf) The Seven Sisters,
near the Skeena River.   17

(Left) *The bald eagle of the Queen Charlotte Islands.*
(Upper) *Morning mist veils Sproat Lake near Port Alberni, Vancouver Island.*
(Lower) *Scene near Wiah Point in the Queen Charlottes.*

21

(Left) Takakkaw Falls in Yoho National Park. (Right) Near Prince Rupert... unspoiled solitude.

22

B.C. Wildlife

(Above) Stone Sheep.

(Top) Cougar or Mountain Lion.
(Centre) Glaucous-winged Gull.
(Lower) Canada Goose and goslings.

British Columbia is noted for its wildlife — it has the greatest abundance of hoofed animals outside Africa. But that wildlife needs protection — from mountain lion to bald eagle — else here too the species will vanish. Fortunately, many people today are finding that hunting with a camera instead of a gun provides deeper and more lasting satisfaction.

(Top) Coyote.
(Lower) *A family of Moose.*

(Top) Golden-mantled Squirrel.
(Lower) Hoary Marmot.

26   *(Top) Mule Deer buck.*
(Lower) Badger.

(Top) Mountain Goats.
(Centre) Big Horn Sheep.
(Lower) Columbia Black-tailed Deer.

(Top) Variegated Fritillary Butterfly.
(Centre) Tufted Puffin.
(Lower) Raccoon.

(Top) Stellar's Jay.
(Lower) Black Bear.

27

(Left)
Mountain
meadow,
Manning
Provincial
Park.
(Right)
Autumn
in the
mountains.
(Right)
Rock slide
near the
Hope-Princeton
highway.

(Upper Left) Riders on the Bar Q Ranch near Ashcroft.
(Lower Left) Quinisco Lake, Cathedral Provincial Park.
(Above) A naturalist explains the law and lore of the forests.
(Right) Emerald Lake, Yoho National Park.

Winter holds in its icy grip the land beyond Fort Nelson, in the northeast.

The Nelson River winds through the frozen stillness of the far north.

Pitt Meadows Range, lower mainland.

Through the Rocky Mountains between Fort St. John and Prince George *(overleaf)* struggled the party led by Alexander Mackenzie, intrepid explorer and fur-trader. From the Peace to the Parsnip to the Fraser River, then fifteen days westward they went to the Bella Coola River and North Bentinck Arm. Mackenzie wrote on a rock, commemorating the first crossing by white men of this continent overland, north of Mexico: "Alexander Mackenzie, from Canada, by land, 22nd of July, 1793."

S.S. Beaver, by Jack Hambleton.

Our Heritage

Searching for the Straits of Anian, a new route to Cathay, the North West Passage between the Atlantic and the Pacific, many daring sea dogs sailed up the British Columbia coast in centuries gone by.

Historians disagree on how far north Francis Drake sailed his Golden Hinde in 1579, but today a 7,219-foot peak on Vancouver Island is named for his ship.

The first recorded white man to go ashore in British Columbia was English Captain James Cook. Seeking a safe harbour in which to repair his masts, Cook entered Nootka Sound in 1778 and anchored in Friendly Cove (*see overleaf*). He was accompanied by two young Englishmen destined for fame — George Vancouver and William Bligh.

In 1792 Captain Vancouver surveyed the Strait of Juan de Fuca, the Fraser delta, Howe Sound, Jervis and Burrard inlets. Seeking the North West Passage, he charted the British Columbia coast almost to Alaska and circumnavigated Vancouver Island. At Nootka, Vancouver found the hospitable Spanish commissioner, Senor Bodega y Quadra, waiting to turn the area over to him. Friendship is the reason Vancouver Island appears on old maps as "Quadra and Vancouver's Island."

Long before the white man's discovery, the country had been home to many tribes of Indians whose cultures were moulded by the environment. Legends, rock carvings, totems and thousands of artifacts remain as a legacy of primitive beginnings. Actually, the totem is now recognized as one of the most highly developed forms of primitive art anywhere in the world.

After the navigators came the land explorers, the fur hunters and voyageurs — Alexander Mackenzie, Simon Fraser, David Thompson, David Stuart, John Finlay and others — most of whom left their names permanently on the Province's lakes or rivers.

Also written large in the annals of British Columbia are two early enterprises — the North West Company and the Hudson's Bay Company. Towns stand today on some of the sites of their forts and trading posts.

March 23, 1858, is the date often credited as the opening day for settlement of this Province. A party of miners, bound for the Thompson River area because of reports of gold, had stopped for lunch near Fort Yale, where the Fraser River boils out of the canyon. Here a casual glance revealed "the richest and longest worked bar" on the Fraser.

The gleam of gold immediately flashed as far south as San Francisco and thousands of other searchers soon swarmed the country. On August 21, 1862, ex-sailor Billy Barker made his fabulous strike on Williams Creek. Ghost towns now haunt the land as eerie reminders of vanished boom towns once bulging and raucous with miners and camp followers.

Only the strong and determined could carve their names with pride as a record of their harsh struggle against the forbidding terrain of mountains and canyons. Two of the Province's early leaders — Sir James Douglas ("father of B.C.") and Sir Matthew Begbie ("the hanging judge") — were as stern and uncompromising as the territory they served.

The photograph of Friendly Cove opposite recalls the ghostly figure of Captain Cook and we unconsciously try to locate his ship. As other phantoms of the past haunt our historical memories, we see Cook trading with five hundred Indians, being rowed around Bligh's Island, then sailing north, blown by a storm outside the Queen Charlottes. We envision other ships coming for sea otter skins, including those of Lieutenant John Meares, British trader, lovable rogue and catalyst in "The Nootka Affair" which almost caused war between England and Spain. In 1788 Meares brought to Nootka fifty Chinese artisans to build and launch British Columbia's first ship, the North West America, under the approving eye of the famous Nootka chief, Maquinna.

Explorers by sea and land, the Indians before them, the fur traders and the gold seekers all wove the web of British Columbia history. They have created a rich and varied tapestry — Our Heritage.

Friendly Cove, Nootka Island, on Vancouver Island's west coast.

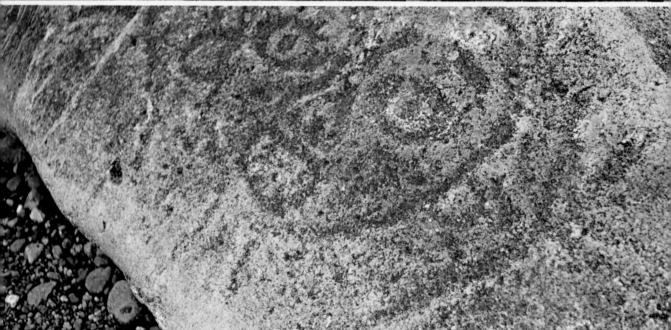

42

(Upper) Church and totem pole at Haida (Old Masset) in the Queen Charlottes.
(Lower) Petroglyph (Indian rock painting), Quadra Island.
(Right) Oldest standing totem pole, Skidegate, Queen Charlottes.

(Left) Totem poles at Kispiox in northwest.
(Above) Bulkley River and coastal mountains.
(Below) 'Ksan Indian Village, near Hazelton.

45

Barkerville

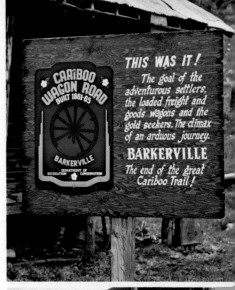

From 1858 on through the 1860s, thousands upon thousands of young men, from California and elsewhere, passed through Victoria and Vancouver, up the Fraser and Thompson Rivers, along the fur brigade trail through the Okanagan Valley, on their way to the fabulous gold fields of the Cariboo.

One of these hopefuls was Billy Barker, a sailor from Cornwall, England, who jumped ship to strike it rich in the typical interior gold mining boomtown which later was named for him, Barkerville, east of Quesnel. The town is now being restored to its former glory of the 1860s, when it had the largest population north of San Francisco and west of Chicago.

Billy Barker's experience parallels that of so many gold-seekers of those days. He toiled his way up the rugged Cariboo Trail, then almost broke his back digging to a depth of forty feet with absolutely no success. However, it was the next two feet that made Billy and his partners wealthy. Alas, Billy lost every cent and died in poverty, but his Barkerville lives again as a restored gold town, attracting many tourists every year.

PAINLESS
TOOTH EXTRACTION
DR. JONES WILL EXTRACT TEETH AND
PERFORM SHORT OPERATIONS WITHOUT PAIN

OFFICE FEE
TEETH EXTRACTED OR $5.00
FILLED WITH GOLD $5.00

Cathedral Grove, by Geoffrey Traunter.

A Forest Empire

In the ancient world, men cut down trees to build their ships and cities and never gave a thought to the future of the forests. As a result many areas around the Mediterranean Sea, for example, have been bare and treeless for several centuries. Once in Africa's northern regions there were lakes, rivers and greenery, where today the sands of the Sahara Desert eternally advance upon the neighbouring territory.

Generations of North Americans hewed down trees to make their canoes, dishes, totem poles, tools, bridges, docks, cabins, fences, cooking fires and, later on, railroad ties, trestles, telephone poles and even mansions.

Gradually the forests were banished from the middle of this continent. In the 1930s dry winds swept across the treeless plains and the world first heard the term "dustbowl." Countless farmers and homesteaders were ruined, forced to sell out and go west to try their luck again.

Almost too late, the human race learned the severe lesson that we are closely and irrevocably dependent upon nature, that we must preserve her system of checks and balances to ensure our own personal survival.

Greedy folk who looted the mountainsides of their "green gold" and left the slopes vulnerable to the forces of erosion have given place to more enlightened people who practice silviculture, the growing of forest trees from seed or seedlings to maturity.

This is especially true in British Columbia, where between 3,000 and 3,500 companies are engaged in logging and manufacturing 5,000 products from logs. In this Province, the influence of the forests on the weather, the livelihood of the people and even their outlook on life is too great to be measured.

Fifty-nine per cent of the Province — an estimated 138,400,000 acres — is covered by basically softwood forests of predominantly coniferous trees, evergreens which keep their leaves or needles for more than one year. Thus, British Columbia contains more than half the marketable timber in Canada in such trees as the hemlock, red cedar, balsam fir, Douglas fir, spruce, lodgepole pine and yellow cedar. This is because the Province is one of the few areas on earth where conditions of climate and soil are ideal for the growth of an abundance of tall, straight trees.

British Columbia's trees live in two different climates on either side of the Coast Mountains. In the mild, wet weather of the western slopes, the country's richest stand of conifers covers 17,800,000 acres. Some of these forest giants soar to two hundred feet or more in height and measure eight feet around the trunk. Some live for hundreds of years. At their roots, on the forest floor, flourish bracken, mosses, ferns, lichens, and scores of flowers.

The inland forest area, east of the Cascade Mountains, is six times larger, covering 107,500,000 acres in the lush interior valleys and even climbing as high as several thousand feet up the mountainsides.

Ninety-five per cent of British Columbia's forest land is owned by the public and managed by the Provincial Government; four per cent is in private hands and the rest is protected by the Federal government for national parks, military establishments, Indian reserves and special uses.

Hunters, campers, sports fishermen, hikers, skiers and other nature lovers leave their frenetic lives in the cities of this Province and escape into the forest solitudes whenever they get a chance. Thousands of miles of roads built in the forests by the logging industry can be used by the public on weekends and holidays when the work of transporting timber out of the woods is not going on. Campsites, picnic grounds and boat launching ramps have been created for the public by several forestry organizations in their own working areas.

Impenetrable primeval forests choked with heavy underbrush, fallen, dead and decaying trees, fungus growth, ideal breeding grounds for pests, do not provide a good home for wildlife. Lightning often solves this kind of problem with a disastrous but cleansing forest fire.

Man's efforts at forest husbandry and planned harvesting create a more attractive environment for the creatures of the woods, by providing breathing space between the trees, new growth for cover and food, and also by curbing forest diseases.

Deer, grouse, elk, raccoon, cougar, wolf, beaver, marten, bear, squirrel, moose, fox, lynx, otter, bobcat, migrant birds and the human animal are all the richer for it in their enjoyment of A Forest Empire.

They all grow on the forest floor.

(Opposite) Spanish Moss.
(Top) Aerial ferns on a tree branch.

(Left) Skunk Cabbage.
(Right) Fungus on a tree bole.

(Top Left) *Trillium.*
(Top Right) *Wild Loganberry flowers.*
(Lower) *Wild Strawberries in bloom.*

The Firs

There is a lonely minor chord that sings
Faintly and far along the forest ways,
When the firs finger faintly on the strings
Of that rare violin the night wind plays,
Just as it whispered once to you and me
Beneath the English pines beyond the sea.

An excerpt from AUTUMN'S ORCHESTRA
(Inscribed to One Beyond Seas) by poet
E. Pauline Johnson, a native Mohawk Indian,
(1862-1913), one of Canada's best-known authors.
She is buried in Stanley Park, Vancouver,
near Lost Lagoon, the subject of one of her
most famous poems.

British Columbia's prosperity rests largely upon the forest industry, which creates 5,000 products from logs — including lumber for building purposes, shingles and shakes for roofs and walls, plywood, veneers, pulpwood, pressed wall panels, fireplace fuel, poles, pilings for docks and foundations of buildings, newsprint . . . and the paper for books like this one.

Before a man in a hard-hat and caulk boots, carrying a single-bit axe and a small power saw can run his experienced eye up and down a Douglas fir, cedar or hemlock, a great deal of activity has to take place on the part of the 30,000 employees of the logging industry's 2,000 companies.

Some of the teamwork necessary to the Province's major industry begins five or ten years before the first "Faller" inspects a tree, judges its soundness and figures out how to fell it without causing damage either to itself or others nearby.

Cameramen take aerial photographs of forest lands, topographic maps of the chosen areas are prepared, engineers study drawings, logging roads have to be blasted out and bull-dozed, bridges have to be built strong enough to bear the weight of the equipment that picks up and carries the logs from the forest, usually to the nearest tidewater.

Rafts, barges, tugs, giant trucks and railroads all transport logs to the mill or log ponds. Floating booms containing hundreds of logs apiece are a common sight along the waterways of the Province. "Strays" line the bathing beaches everywhere, and have to be retrieved.

Since the first sawmill was built near Victoria in 1848, this Province has become a world-wide trader in lumber, with nearly 900 sawmills employing almost 23,000 people. More than 80 per cent of the lumber produced is exported.

Pulp mills use pulpwood and chips from local sawmills, as well as decadent stands of trees and timber left in areas which have been "logged off."

The wood products industry also includes shingle mills, paper mills, plywood and veneer plants, and accounts for a large part of British Columbia's factory shipments.

(Left) Cutting the tree.

(Top) Building a forest road.
(Lower) Loading trucks with logs.

65

Mainstay of British Columbia's economy, the forest yields products which are in demand in numerous other countries. Unlike this Province's mineral resources, the forests are perpetually renewable by good management and constant re-planting, much like any other valu-able crop.

Foresters have already planted 415 million new trees throughout British Columbia. By the end of this year, the total should be 490 million baby trees in the ground. Govern-ment and industry have set a goal of 150 million seedlings planted on 400,000 acres *every year* by 1980. Mother Nature, who plants millions of embryo trees herself, has given us no official figures on her aims. Be-cause of this renewing of the forests, British Columbia is said to have more trees today than existed two hundred years ago.

C.P.R. track laying near Rogers Pass, 1885, by Rudy Kovach.

The Growing Giant

The rapid growth of British Columbia cities and industries could be likened to the growth of her trees. From the tiny seed of the towering cedar a sapling springs, and over the years its crown reaches for the sun until it takes its place among the other giants of the forest.

Even in its unpretentious beginnings and with the massive barrier of the Rocky Mountains separating the region from the rest of Canada, our forebears believed in the future of this Province as a prime source of natural wealth.

To open up the country and develop its resources, a transportation link through the Rockies was imperative. When this was achieved, further feats were accomplished until the Province was criss-crossed by railroads and highways.

Many hardy and courageous men contributed their lives and skills in engineering firsts and the seemingly impossible became reality. Vast mountains had been tunnelled, mighty rivers spanned and roads carved in their rugged canyons. The deep-sea ports of Vancouver, New Westminster, Victoria and Prince Rupert could finally offer the goods of the rest of Canada to the Pacific world.

The economy of British Columbia is underpinned by power. To meet the continued rapid industrial and population growth in the Province, B.C. Hydro predicts an annual increase of 9.3 per cent in the demand for electric power. Major generating sites will add 2.5 million kilowatts by the end of 1977, an increase of more than 60 percent from the 4.4 million kilowatts available today. Two of the projects — Peace River and Mica — are among the world's biggest hydro-electric developments.

Typical of the Province's vigorous mineral industry are the operations of Placer Development Limited, a Canadian-owned company headquartered in Vancouver. It operates two copper mines and a molybdenum mine (the world's second largest), which jointly ship in excess of 175 million pounds of metal annually.

Another major industry, of course, is fishing which last year returned its professional Izaak Waltons more money than ever before in history — the value of landed fish was nearly $74 million.

The B.C. Government ferry fleet is the world's fastest growing, with 26 ships on thirteen separate runs. It carried 7.5 million passengers last year, a tenfold increase in little more than twelve years.

B.C. Telephone serves over 1.1 million units throughout the Province. There are more telephones per capita in Vancouver than in any other city in Canada — 70 phones per 100 people.

We have timber and cement to build the cities of the future; minerals to produce the machines and materials in the manufacture of a plethora of goods for ourselves and the world; and an abundance of power to activate the industries of today and tomorrow. British Columbia has come far since Captain George Vancouver set foot upon this land, yet all we have is just a promise of what is yet to come. Along our broad horizons a new and more exciting era stretches before our eager eyes.

Everything seems big in British Columbia. The mountains, the rivers and the Pacific Ocean stimulate the people to think on a grand scale. This expansive optimism means that more businesses are born and die here than in any other province of Canada. The challenge and the gamble are perpetual, and a constant flood of new settlers eager to take a chance is convincing proof.

What the newcomer finds is a country of startling contrasts — modern city life right next to the raw outdoors. Bears and deer are frequent night visitors to the gardens while the owners may be attending the latest opera or play.

From relatively slow progress in the first half of this century, British Columbia launched itself into the markets of the world, making huge strides in its economy that surpassed the expectations of most. Today we can say that we are both witnesses of and participants in The Growing Giant.

Fireworks at the Vancouver Sea Festival.

Aerial shot, part of Greater Vancouver.

72

Vancouver

Canada's third largest city is named after Captain George Vancouver, R.N. Its first white settler was a saloon-keeper named "Gassy Jack" (he talked a lot) Deighton, who brought his Indian wife, a yellow dog and a barrel of whiskey to brighten the lives of the millhands and sailors on Burrard Inlet by opening a bar. The infant community was called Gastown in his honour. But before either of these Englishmen arrived, several Indian villages existed within the future city limits.

Vancouver today would astound both the captain and the saloon-keeper. From ocean shore to mountain top almost a million people enjoy the superb setting, claimed to rival that of Rio de Janeiro. Here in this modern metropolis of the Pacific, life can be as rich, varied and exciting as the primeval environment. Vancouver's world-wide fame draws millions of visitors from this continent and abroad every year, and many return to stay forever.

When words fail to express, pictures can sometimes convey. On the following pages is a sampling of the colourful attractions of Greater Vancouver today.

(Left) English Bay.
(Top Right) Downtown business section, North Shore Mountains.
(Lower Right) A corner of Stanley Park.

(Overleaf) The Swimmer statue, Stanley Park; Killer Whale, Aquarium; Sailboats, West Vancouver; Sun-worshippers on a Vancouver beach.

Vancouver:
Major Art Centre

Seventeen terracotta sculpture models — made by Michelangelo Buonarroti (1475-1564) personally or "attributed" to him or his workshop — exhibited in Vancouver's Planetarium Museum during the winter of 1972-1973, signalled the emergence of this city as a major art centre.

Nine are actually from the hand of the great sculptor, and only 33 such models still exist in the world. The subjects are studies for Medici tombs in Florence and various church statues in Rome *(Top Left)*. These models belong to a private collector in Vancouver, who shared them with the public (in eight Canadian cities, courtesy Rothmans Ltd.) but preferred to remain anonymous.

The mild climate and the grandeur of its scenery have attracted many artists from all over the world to settle in British Columbia. Their work fills the many art galleries in Vancouver and is shown regularly near the Aquarium *(Lower Left)* in Stanley Park.

(Right) Ship in English Bay, awaiting a free berth in Burrard Inlet.

Port of Vancouver

First cargo to leave the Port of Vancouver was a load of lumber in 1864. Today ships of every type and size ply the waters of Burrard Inlet, focus of Western Canada's trade with the world. Dozens of laden freighters, many carrying enough lumber to build over 1,000 average homes, clear the Port each year — enough in total weight to rank as the second largest shipment next to grain. Powerful tugs maneuver among ponderous freighters and sleek passenger vessels, assisting with docking and departure. More than 20,000 visits are paid to the Port annually by deepsea and coastal vessels.

(Left Top) Typical modern steel-hulled tugboat, English Bay.
(Lower Left) Self-loading barge, Queen Charlotte Islands.

Spirit of London, passenger ship of the P&O Lines.

University of British Columbia

The University of British Columbia, begun in 1915, has an incomparable setting on Point Grey, Vancouver, and is the Province's largest. Twenty-five thousand students are doing undergraduate and postgraduate work in nearly all major disciplines in 300 permanent buildings.

Thousands of visitors tour the one thousand acres of the campus every year to see, among other attractions, the Rose Garden, the Japanese charm of the Nitobe Garden, and Totem Park's art works by the Kwakiutl and Haida Indians of the Province.

These artifacts will be part of the Museum of Man, the university's anthropological complex designed by Vancouver architect, Arthur Erickson, which is to be completed and open to the public before April, 1975.

Many thousands of artifacts will be exhibited from the University's own collection of local Indian art, the Koerner collection of tribal master-works, and the Borden collection of excavated treasures dating back to prehistoric times in British Columbia.

They will be displayed in a recreation of a typical coastal Indian village, between the forest and the sea, as it was before the arrival of the first white people in this area.

(Left) Aerial view of the University of British Columbia campus. 83

Victoria the City

Captain William H. McNeill of the Hudson's Bay Company explored the southern tip of Vancouver Island in 1837 and found a safe harbour the Songhees Indians called "Camosun," meaning "the rush of waters." With Fort Vancouver on the Columbia River about to be taken over by the Americans, James Douglas came up on the H.B.C.'s *Beaver*, the North Pacific's first steamer *(See Page 38)* to found a new fur-trading post. It was built in 1843 and named Fort Victoria in honour of the British queen.

Today named simply Victoria, this city has been the capital of the Province since the union with Canada in 1871. Said to be "A Bit of Old England," Victoria is famous for many British touches . . . tea and crumpets at the Empress Hotel *(Right)*, cricket, a leisurely way of life, the horse-drawn Tallyhos and double-decker London buses *(Page 87)* that carry tourists from stately mansion to tweed and sweetshops, to the refurbished Victorian City Hall *(See Page 88)*, the reconstructed Centennial Square. They pass gardens as colourful as those in Blighty and lamp-standards adorned with hanging baskets of flowers, just like in a British seaside resort — which Victoria closely resembles.

Among the area population of about 175,000, many are retired folk from many lands enjoying Canada's mildest climate. The population goes up when the legislators are working in the Parliament Buildings *(See Page 89)*, and when the session ends it drops. In summer it rises to dramatic heights during the tourist season.

The Provincial Museum *(See Page 87)* covers all aspects of pioneer days, from Indians whale-hunting to dioramas of local animals, from a gold-hunter's pan to the many-buttoned kid gloves and boots of a turn-of-the-century matron. These days are recalled in Bastion Square, too, on the site of the original Fort Victoria, which area once echoed to the shouts of gold seekers bound for the Cariboo and the Klondike. Then it declined into a "skid road" and now is reborn with good restaurants, boutiques and the Maritime Museum. Nearby Trounce Alley *(Page 86)* is named for the man who used to own it.

(Right) Aerial view of the Inner Harbour, showing the Parliament Buildings and the Empress Hotel.

(Left) Trounce Alley,
all nostalgia and
gaslight.

(Top) Courtyard of the Provincial Museum.
(Lower) A horse-drawn Tallyho and a genuine London bus   87
carry sight-seers around Victoria.

Craigflower Manor-Farm, first occupied in 1856, is a fine example of early colonial architecture.

(Top) Indian display in the Provincial Muse
(Lower) Victoria's refurbished City Hall.
(Right) Parliament Buildings from the Inner Harb

(Above) Mrs. Robert Pym Butchart hated the sight of the gaping hole in the earth, north of Victoria, after her husband's cement company had taken the limestone out. In 1904 the Butcharts began to plan the exquisite Sunken Gardens. The English Rose Garden, the Japanese and Italian Gardens followed – the famous Butchart Gardens of today.

(Right) Hatley Castle, fifty-roomed greystone mansion built as the home of the James Dunsmuirs after they left Government House in 1909, is now the property of the three armed services and is known as Royal Roads Military College.

New Westminster

Every May, during the "Hyack" Festival in New Westminster on the Fraser River, an unusual salute to Queen Victoria's birthday is fired, using the humble anvil instead of a cannon. It was Victoria who personally chose the new city's name — after "Queenborough" and "Queensborough" had been briefly considered — for the then capital of the mainland colony of British Columbia. A year and a half after the British Columbia and Vancouver Island colonies united, the colony's capital became Victoria. However, New Westminster is still proudly called "The Royal City" unofficially.

In 1973, New Westminster bathed in the glory of being host (with Burnaby) to the Canada Summer Games. The city also offers history at Irving House, an authentically-furnished Victorian home and museum, Oriental beauty in the Japanese Friendship Garden, a huge Childrens' May Day Festival, fishing along the Fraser River, and all the movement and excitement of a major port.

The famous anvil salute opens the "Hyack" Festival in May (Above). The Garden of Friendship (Right) was officially opened by Mayor Masataka Kizaki, of the city of Moriguchi, Osaka, Japan, in 1963.

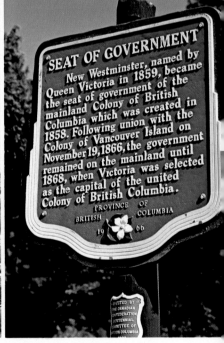

SEAT OF GOVERNMENT

New Westminster, named by Queen Victoria in 1859, became the seat of government of the mainland Colony of British Columbia which was created in 1858. Following union with the Colony of Vancouver Island on November 19, 1866, the government remained on the mainland until 1868, when Victoria was selected as the capital of the united Colony of British Columbia.

PROVINCE OF
BRITISH COLUMBIA
1966

(Top) Aerial view of New Westminster.
(Left) Historic Irving House.

(Top) Hyack Festival Parade in May.
(Lower) The City Hall.

Heritage Village.

Burnaby

Burnaby, directly east of Vancouver, is the most populous municipality in the Province, with 132,000 people. In 1973 (with New Westminster) Burnaby was host to the Canada Summer Games, and Burnaby Lake was the scene of the aquatic events. From Simon Fraser University, one of Canada's newest, *(See p. 99)* there is a magnificent view of Vancouver, Burrard Inlet, the North Shore and Indian Arm. Other highlights not to be missed are Century Gardens Park, famed for rhododendrons, Central Park, the largest of Burnaby's parks, and Heritage Village, which shows life as it was lived here eighty years ago *(Left)*.

Burnaby Art Gallery is within a large old home, the Ceperley Mansion (See p. 98).

Crowning Burnaby Mountain is the starkly modern Simon Fraser University.

Children often play on this free form sculpture on the shore of Deer Lake.

North Vancouver

The City and District Municipality of North Vancouver stretch along Burrard Inlet and the North Shore. The city's story began around 1860 with a sawmill later sold to Sewell Prescott Moody, after whom the settlement was named Moodyville. In 1890, when Moodyville was the only community north of San Francisco with electric lights, it was discovered that twin peaks up above resembled seated lions, so the harbour entrance became known as "The Lions Gate." Site of the largest shipyards in the Province, North Vancouver sends out ships laden with lumber, grain, sulphur and manufactured goods. Spectacular views can be enjoyed from two ski areas — Mount Seymour, where the road winds up to a 3,000 foot elevation, and Grouse Mountain, where The Skyride whisks you 3,700 feet up in just a few minutes.

(Top) Aerial view of North Vancouver's industrial section.
(Lower) The shipyards.

Capilano Canyon suspension bridge.

The pleasant murmur of Lynn Creek.

In North Vancouver there are suspension bridges to scare you delightfully in both Capilano Canyon Park and Lynn Canyon Park *(opposite)*, areas renowned for natural beauty. The Park and Tilford Gardens *(above)* show what man can do to improve the attractiveness of an industrial site. Ranging from the Oriental to the rose and native woods and from the full summer blooms to the brilliant lighting effects of the Christmas and New Year season, the seven different gardens offer something for every plant admirer. The areas are compressed and cleverly merged to give an impression of much greater space than actually exists.

Year-round beauty is intensified to mark public holidays at Park and Tilford's (seven, in all) Gardens.

West Vancouver

Highrise apartments line Burrard Inlet among the "posh" shopping districts of Park Royal, Ambleside and Dundarave, in West Vancouver, on the seaward side of Lions Gate Bridge. Private homes of ever-increasing cost edge the shore and climb the mountains. On four thousand acres the Guinness family of beer and stout fame purchased in the thirties stand some of the largest and most opulent houses in Greater Vancouver. To serve their holdings, now known as The British Properties, the Guinnesses built Lions Gate Bridge. Lighthouse Park *(Below)* at Point Atkinson offers hiking trails through coastal forestland. The large marina called Fisherman's Cove is the site of the West Vancouver Yacht Club. Not far away is attractive Whytecliff Park on the way to Horseshoe Bay on Howe Sound, from where ferries leave for Nanaimo *(See page 107),* the Sunshine Coast and Bowen Island.

(Right) Aerial view of West Vancouver.

106
(Top) West Vancouver is the gateway to Garibaldi Park with its wild beauty and alpine flowers.
(Lower) Capilano Golf Course, near the British Properties.

A B.C. ferry on the way from Horseshoe Bay to Nanaimo,
one link in an extensive system.

108   The sunshine coast offers year-round recreation.
Islands and sounds await those who want to fish,
gather oysters, golf, swim, sail, or laze in the sun.

(Top) Gibsons Landing.
(Lower) Sechelt.

(Top Left) A successful charter.
(Top Right) Pender Harbour.
(Lower) Beach Gardens Resort Hotel,
Powell River.

109

Richmond

Nearly all of Richmond Municipality is on two islands. Sea Island contains Vancouver International Airport, one of the country's largest. Lulu Island recalls Miss Lulu Sweet, an actress who charmed the pioneers when she came here with the first theatrical company to visit this province. Two schools of thought exist on how Richmond received its name — either from the favourite place in Australia of a certain farmer's daughter, or from the home town in Yorkshire, England, of the wife of the first reeve of Richmond, B.C.

Because it is on the rich soil of the Fraser River delta, Richmond possesses much farmland, some of which is being chewed up by "progress." The fishing community of Steveston is there, too. Many of the men who catch the fish and the women who work in the canneries are of Japanese descent. The local meeting place for all races, The Martial Arts Centre, and the Buddhist Church feature roofs curved and pointed in Japanese style, oriental lamps and landscaping.

(Left) The centre of Richmond from the air.

Over the North Pole, spanning the Pacific, all across Canada and down south of the border, airlines link Vancouver's International Airport with the whole world. (Top) Canadian Pacific Airlines. (Lower) Air Canada.

(Top Right) The George C. Reifel Waterfowl Refuge near Delta, south of Richmond. (Lower Right) Salmon fishing boat from the air.

Fraser Valley

Millions of years of silt washing down from the mountains created a hundred miles of arable land at the mouth of the Fraser River, for the raising of cattle, fruit and vegetables. Salmon fishing, truck farming, the dairy industry are here, too, in the valley named for Simon Fraser *(See also p. 134)*, fur-trader and explorer, in 1813. The Hudson's Bay Company established Fort Langley in 1827. Through the Fort in the 1850s streamed thousands of miners when gold was discovered on the Fraser River.

(Right) Fraser River Valley from the air.
(Left) Fort Langley.

114

Nanaimo

Started as a joke in 1967, Nanaimo's annual Bathtub Race has become an international event. (The name Nanaimo comes from the Sne-ny-mo Indians.) In real bathtubs propelled by engines of no more than six horse-power, hundreds dare thirty-six miles across the Strait of Georgia to Kitsilano Beach in Vancouver. In Nanaimo Harbour is 760-acre Newcastle Island Park, once a source of coal and sandstone, now full of woodland trails, playing fields and picnic grounds. Nanaimo is the gateway city to provincial parks like Strathcona and English-man River Falls, the forest beauty of Cathedral Grove *(See p. 50)*, as well as Port Hardy and Campbell River.

(Top Left) Campbell River fishing fleet.
(Lower Left) Nanaimo.
(Top) Cape Mudge Lighthouse.
(Right) Little Qualicum Falls.

(Lower
Penticton airport
(Right
Penticton Peach Festival
(Lower Left
Okanagan Game Farm
(Lower Right
B.C. Square Dance
Jamboree

Penticton

Okanagan School of the Arts meets in Penticton each year to study dancing, pottery-making, writing, painting, astronomy, music and native Indian crafts. Early in August, the Penticton Peach Festival is held, with five days of parades, dancing, singing, variety entertainments, a beef barbecue, an art show, beauty queens, Scottish pipers, car racing, rugby games, logging exhibitions and an air show. Everywhere lurk the Peach Fuzz, waiting to haul off to jail anyone caught not wearing a Festival badge. Before the Peach Festival excitement has time to fade, the B.C. Square Dance Jamboree begins, with the downtown streets closed for the five-day celebration.

118

Kelowna

Kelowna, largest city in the Okanagan Valley, is famous for apples *(Top)*, and also for the Annual International Regatta, which is 67 years old and attended by more than 62,000. Five days full of pageantry, entertainment and thrills include daring, one-man kite-flying *(Left Top)* over Okanagan Lake *(Left Lower)*.

The Fintry Queen *(Page 120)*, a diesel-powered paddle-wheeler, carries passengers up and down the lake and, when berthed in Kelowna, is a restaurant-cabaret.

Kamloops

Kamloops, whose population jumped in May, 1973, from 28,000 to 60,000 when the city amalgamated with the neighbouring areas, is the bustling centre of a great outdoors country *(Top)*. Known to the Indians as "Cumcloups" or "meeting place," Fort Kamloops *(Above)* was founded by David Stuart, fur-trader, in 1812, near the confluence of the North and South Thompson Rivers. Modern Kamloops is seen *(Left)* from the air.

123

Northern Triangle

In a far northwest triangle are Prince Rupert, Terrace and Kitimat. Prince Rupert received its name as the result of a competition held by the Grand Trunk Pacific Railway (now part of the Canadian National), which chose the place as the western terminus of its line across Canada. George Little, one of the first pre-emptors of land, in 1905 named Terrace because of the terraces of land rising from the Skeena River. The Kitimat Indians, "the people of the snow," gave their name to Kitimat and the Hudson's Bay Company adopted it. Port Simpson, just north of Prince Rupert (*Page 125*) is named for Capt. Aemilius Simpson, founder of Fort Simpson, formerly Fort Nass.

(Left) Totem poles at Prince Rupert.

(Top) Aerial view of Prince Rupert.
(Lower Left) Welcome to Kitimat.
(Lower Right) Fishing off Port Simpson.

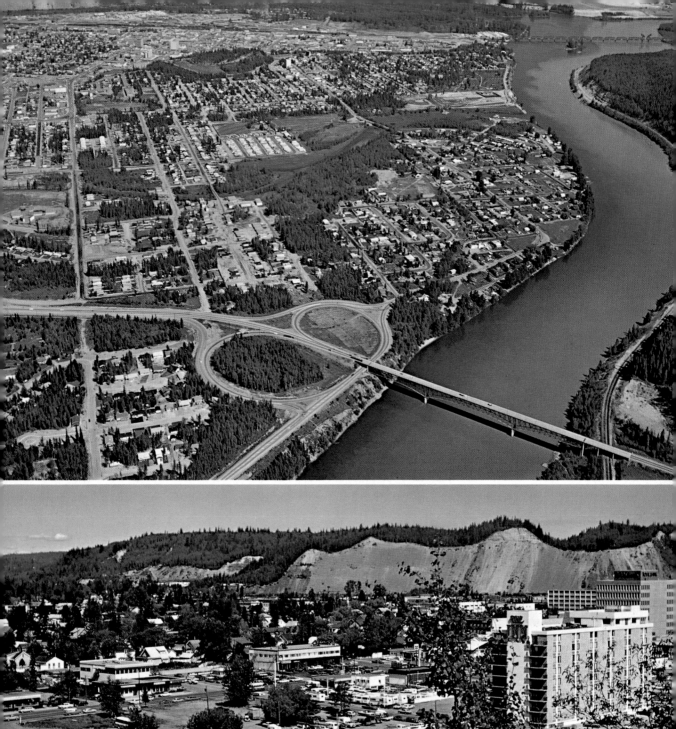

Prince George

Prince George, near the Rocky Mountains, where the Fraser and Nechako Rivers meet, was formerly called Fort George. In 1807 it was founded by Simon Fraser, who named it after George III, the reigning monarch. On the old site now stands Fort George Museum. This is in the ancient homeland of the Carrier Indians. Prince George is now a modern bustling centre serving the needs of an area population of 60,000.

(Left) Prince George.
(Top Right) Fort George Museum.
(Centre) Unique headstones
of the Carrier Indians.
(Lower Right) W.A.C. Bennett Dam.

127

Fort St. John, Fort Nelson and Dawson Creek

Across the northeastern corner of the Province, above Fort St. John, runs the Alaska Highway. Near the modern Fort St. John and the Alberta border, the original fort, Rocky Mountain House, was built in 1798. Today, known for oil drilling and grain production, Fort St. John is probably the oldest white settlement on the mainland of the Province. Fort Nelson, farther north yet, produces natural gas and calls to mind the name of British naval hero of Trafalgar fame, Horatio Nelson. Largest community in the area is Dawson Creek, with a population of 12,500, located at Mile 0 on the Alaska Highway.

(Left) An oil derrick.
(Top Right) Fort St. John in winter.
(Lower Right) Dawson Creek.

128

The smelter city of Trail.

The Kootenays

The Kootenays, East and West, contain some of the most spectacular vistas in British Columbia. This region is noted for its mountains and lakes, reminding many people of the natural charms of Switzerland. The Selkirk, Purcell and Slocan Ranges and the Kootenay and Arrow Lakes unfold hundreds of miles of stunning scenery, and other water and landscapes on a lesser scale have equal appeal. An area with industrial vigour as well as scenic beauty, the Kootenays pulsate with power from the Columbia, Pend d'Oreille and Kootenay Rivers and the largest city Trail (population 15,000) is the abode of the world's biggest non-ferrous smelter. Other leading communities are Nelson, named after the Hon. Hugh Nelson, an early Lieutenant-Governor; Kimberley, which is said to be a namesake of the South African diamond mining centre; and Cranbrook, called after the little Kentish town. Kootenay itself comes from the Indian tribe whose name is derived from "co," meaning "water," and "Tinneh," meaning "people."

(Top Right) Columbia Valley in the East Kootenay.
(Lower right) The frontier town of Fort Steele.

(Above) Alpine flowers in the Bugaboo Mountains.
(Top Left) The city of Nelson on Kootenay Lake.
(Lower Left) The town of Golden on the Kicking Horse River,
with the Selkirk Mountains as a backdrop.

Simon Fraser near Hellsgate Canyon, 1808, by Peter Ewart.

Pathfinders of Today

Silently the canoe parts the blue and limpid waters of the lake, paddles transgress the ever-growing circles, and all is quiet among the shore pines. . .

At this same moment in the far distant city a man, wife and their children are busy loading the station wagon for their annual holiday in the mountains. . .

On the west coast, clinging to the rocks, a scientist laden with a camera is trying to approach a peregrine falcon's nest for a closer view. . .

Every day of the year regardless of the seasons, somebody somewhere is answering the call of the wild in pursuit of his particular hobby or just plainly enjoying himself in the magnificent outdoors.

Fishermen, hunters and campers can escape into the splendour of the land out of sight and sound of each other.

We term them pathfinders of today, more sophisticated and better equipped, but still following the solitary miles of nature and many times paying the penalty for their mistakes.

Canada and British Columbia were leaders in developing a special breed of men in aviation — bush pilots and their sometimes eccentric planes. Besides opening new frontiers in the north, they performed many deeds in defiance of the law of self-preservation — flying in all kinds of weather, grazing cliffs on rescue missions, or dropping supplies in a treacherous canyon to starving trappers.

Highways, railroads and airlines bring modern adventurers closer to their goals in comfort, but arduous terrain lonely and raw still can confront them at journey's end.

Seventeen thousand miles of coastline attract thousands of boat owners to explore sounds, coves and islands for fishing, crabbing, clam digging, oyster gathering and beach cookouts.

Scuba diving in clear waters during the summer, or skiing on the salubrious slopes of high mountains in the winter, have generated their own enthusiastic followers, perhaps surpassed only by the birdwatching fraternity to which anyone in British Columbia can belong.

When the rains drench the Pacific Coast and the silent snowflakes drape the interior valleys in white ermine, the thoughts of many return to summer days. Maps appear on family tables and great adventure plans unfold for the next season. Again this irresistible call of the wild tugs our hearts and again we become the Pathfinders of Today.

(Above) Long Beach, Vancouver Island.   *(Top Right) Canoeing on Deer Lake, Burnaby*

(Centre) Fishing near Smithers, Yellowhead Highway
(Lower Right) Today's pathfinder is the versatile helicopter

138
(Top) Annual Swiftsure Classic Races, Victoria.
(Left) The Bathtub Races at Nanaimo.
(Right) Feeding the ducks on Lost Lagoon, Stanley Park, Vancouver.

(Top) Buying pelts from a typical northern trapper.
(Lower) At Fort Nelson, the annual dog races are
a real endurance test for man and beast.

Very rarely is there a freeze-up in the mild Vancouver winter, but these children are enjoying the temporary skating rink near the Planetarium, and ignoring the view of the West End.

*Taking a spill at the annual
Bulkley Valley Stampede, near the
Hazelton Mountains and Smithers.*

141

We have journeyed to the far reaches of this great Province.
Without moving from our chair we have climbed lofty peaks,
sauntered through remote villages, warmed our bare feet in the
sands of isolated beaches, or watched cowboys eating dust in
rodeos. This is an unspoiled land which haunts us with the
eternal lure of exploration, yet so vast that our minds can
scarcely grasp it. This is the country we call home and where
most of us intend to stay and prosper. We have an abiding joy
in our mountains, rivers, lakes and forests. This is our
British Columbia.

142

Index:

Special photographic credits:

John Smith: pages 22,30 (upper), 31 (right), 132 (lower).
Alma H. Carmichael: pages 24,25,26,27 (left centre, lower right).
William Clark: page 27 (upper left).
Wilfred N. Ray, Neonex International Ltd.: page 123 (upper right).
H.D. von Tiesenhausen: pages 28,29,35,123 (lower).
S.R. Cannings: page 30 (upper), 31 (lower left).
Redivo Photography Ltd., Penticton: page 30 (lower),
31 (lower left), 119 (upper and lower right).
Jack Lindsay: page 81.
Gary Otte: page 127 (lower right).
Hal Bavin: page 131 (upper).
John Bryan: page 133.
Clifford A. Fenner: page 132 (upper).
Willem Roozeboom: page 138 (upper and lower left).
Gerhard T. Kahrmann: Page 131 (lower).

Contents:

This volume was designed by Geoffrey Traunter.
Cameras used by Ted Czolowski were:
Nikon F and Nikon F2.
Film: Eastman Kodak's Kodachrome II
and Kodachrome X.
Paintings on pages 38, 50, 68, 134 by kind
permission of Ocean Construction Supplies Ltd.
'The Firs' from 'Flint and Feather' by E. Pauline Johnson,
courtesy Hodder and Stoughton Limited, Toronto.
Typesetting is by Photype Centre Ltd.,
Colour duplicates, Commercial Illustrators Ltd.,
Colour separations, Quality Separations Ltd.,
Lithography, Agency Press Ltd., all of Vancouver,
British Columbia.